The Poetry Bible

Peter Dainty

Illustrated by Melody-Anne Lee

kevin mayhew

kevin mayhew

First published in Great Britain in 2009 by Kevin Mayhew Ltd
Buxhall, Stowmarket, Suffolk IP14 3BW
Tel: +44 (0) 1449 737978 Fax: +44 (0) 1449 737834
E-mail: info@kevinmayhewltd.com

www.kevinmayhew.com

9 8 7 6 5 4 3 2 1 0

ISBN 978 1 84867 174 4
Catalogue No. 1501182

Illustrations, design and cover by Melody-Anne Lee
Edited by Alison Evans

Printed and bound in Great Britain

Contents

About the author

After studying church history whilst training for the Methodist ministry, Peter Dainty was ordained in 1963 and ministered in two circuits (Brigg and Pontefract). He moved to Bury St Edmunds in 1971 to teach at Culford School (an independent Methodist co-educational boarding and day school), where he stayed until his retirement in 2001. From 1973–1993 he was a non-stipendiary minister at a small church in Bury St Edmunds.

Peter has worked part-time as an editor for Kevin Mayhew Ltd since 1995 and has published: *The Electric Gospel* (poetry), *40 Days, Ready for Christmas?* and *What is Man* (study courses), as well as compiling anthologies: *Circle of Blessings* and six gift books for special occasions, all of which include his own prayers.

Peter is married to Margaret and they have three children and five grandchildren.

Preface

I first started writing poetry for use in worship in 1971, when I came to live in Suffolk. As a Methodist minister and teacher I was looking for something suitable for Christmas services and my supply of Christmas poetry books was rather meagre. Most of what I had to hand was either sentimental, childish, old-fashioned or obscure (to me at any rate). What I was looking for was something which could be understood when read aloud, was in modern language and terminology and related the Christmas story to modern life. With some hesitation I tried to write something myself, and found it was appreciated by the congregations I shared it with.

Over the next two decades I built up quite a collection of such poems and used them successfully in local churches, and also in church magazines. By then I had written material not only for Christmas but also for other seasons of the Christian year, until eventually I had a lot of poems, especially about Jesus, and based on the Gospels.

In the late nineties Kevin Mayhew encouraged me to put them together in a book and this was published in 2000 under the title *The Electric Gospel*. The idea for the title was based on the thought that just as the modern world depends so much on electricity to keep it going, so the Gospel of Jesus Christ has given the world spiritual and moral energy for 2000 years. And we still need that power today.

The Electric Gospel sold so well that Kevin asked me to write a sequel. By this time I had written many more poems based not just on the Gospels, but on other parts of the Bible too; so the result was the publication of *The Electric Bible* in 2003. This was followed by *The Electric Bible revised and enlarged* in 2005. It contained all my previous poems plus 38 new items (15 poems and 23 prayers).

Now I am delighted that this new edition has been published, enhanced by the striking illustrations of Melody-Anne Lee.

I am grateful for the encouragement and support I've always received from Kevin Mayhew, and also from my wife, Margaret, who would never let me put the work away in a drawer and forget about it.

Peter Dainty

Let there be light

Genesis 1:3

'Let there be light,' says God,
and his word
speeds through dark chaos
on streams of fire,
hanging the emptiness
with spinning multitudes
of blazing lanterns,
until all space glows.

For God is light,
and he must radiate
in rising suns
and in volcanic fire;
in subterranean caves
where phosphorous gleams,
and in the darting firefly's tropic night.

Let all things shine,
and darkness be the backcloth only
of God's dreams.

But that crude light we see with fleshy eyes
is simply the beginning
of far brighter visions.
There is a spirit-light of truth and love,
a light displayed, not in the world of things,
but in the human soul –
the candle of the Lord;
a holy radiance,
which reveals the mystery
of the being of God
and lights this earth
with heaven.

The world is not transfigured
by our paler imitations of the sun –
glaring electric power
that drives the demons
only from the surface of our minds
to lurk in its subconscious caverns.
But we must seek that inner light,
that pure and shadowless flame,
which leaves no hiding place
for hate or fear.
We may dismiss it
as the stuff of haloes
and of angels' wings,
but it alone can guide us
to a dazzling destiny
in God.

God's marriage blessing

Genesis 2:23, 24

Let love rule in your lives,
and make you one.
Let love rule everything –
all joys and pleasures,
and all grief and pain;
times of excitement and delight,
and the everyday routine.
Let love rule in your minds,
that all your thoughts
be for the other's good,
and not their ill.

Let love reign in your bodies,
so that you may share your passions
with an equal ecstasy,
but share them with no other.
And if love truly reigns within your hearts,
though trials come
which tempt you both to part,
you never will.
So let love rule,
and you'll know then,
that I'll be with you both,
for evermore. Amen.

The voice of the serpent

Genesis 3:1-9

If the innocent woman of Eden
could suddenly hear
the voice of the serpent
coming from nowhere,
and tempting her
to defy the will of God,
how much more can we
less innocent ones
still hear
the subtle serpent's
seductive whisper
calling us
from the dark undergrowth
of our unsuspecting minds?

'Surely your freedom must not be denied.
If God knows best, then you,
made in his image,
must be allowed to know
as much as he.

The truth is beautiful,
and knowledge is so sweet.
Just taste and see.
It is a lie to say
that ignorance is bliss.
God seeks to keep control
and must impose this prohibition
on the human soul;
or it is God who'll die,
not you.
Throw off his chains.
Show that the human spirit reigns.
Let all the earth rejoice
in mankind's better world!'

Thus speaks the serpent's voice;
and we, renouncing God,
now labour to produce
a better life,
at least for some.
But lust and pride have led
to hate and fear,
and poverty, injustice,
greed and war remain.
Yet, hiding from our God
in guilt and shame,
can we not hear,
even at this late hour,
not now the serpent's poisonous hiss,
but God's more passionate, searching call:
'People of earth,
where are you?'

After the flood

Genesis 6:5–9:17

God led Noah safely through the flood,
from the plains of Mesopotamia
to the mountains of Ararat.
It was a voyage between two worlds –
from the primitive world
of myth and legend,
the world of gods and giants,
into the world we know
and now inhabit,
the world of rules and rulers.

Eden's age of innocence
(so the story goes)
had given way,
to an unruly age
of violence
and corruption.
But the great flood
put an end to all that.
And after the flood,
there was law
based on strict justice –
a life for a life.
It was the beginning
of social order and control,
and we, the descendants of Noah,
have inherited his world,
although we've come a long way
since then.

Even the animals
were now ruled by fear.
Their flesh could be eaten,
and their bodies offered
in sacrifice.
Yet the eating of blood
was forbidden,
because the blood was the life,
and all life was sacred.
But we've come a long way
since then.

Continued overleaf

By the rainbow covenant,
God promised
the stability of nature –
enough to make possible
the unsteady growth
of human civilisation.
'Never again,' said God,
'will I destroy
all living creatures;
and seedtime and harvest,
cold and heat,
summer and winter,
day and night
will remain
as long as the earth endures.'
Oh glorious promise!

And we can surely trust God
not to break that promise.
The worry now is –
because we've come a long way
since the days of Noah,
can we trust *ourselves*
not to break God's promise
for him?

Moving on

Genesis 12:1-9; Hebrews 11:8-10, 13-16

Abraham was called by God
to leave his home
among the nations
and to seek a better land –
a city that was built
on God's foundations.

So Abraham moved on,
not settling down
to die in Haran
like his father,
but shaking off the past
in searching for God's future.

Always travelling on,
he lived in tents,
a stranger and a refugee
even in Canaan.
He was to become
the father of all
those restless, wandering
and dissatisfied ones
who, like him, were haunted
by the persistent nudging
of the living God.

Abraham's descendants
are as countless as the stars –
pilgrims of the spirit,
and pioneers of faith,
whom God has chosen
to keep on moving on,
until at last
they find their home
in God's eternal kingdom.

Jacob

Genesis 28:10-22; 32:22-32

Twice God spoke to Jacob
in the desert night –
once as he slept and dreamed,
once as he fought till morning light.

Jacob the deceiver
fled to a desert land
he made a rock his pillow,
his bed was the stony sand.

But God is always with us,
wherever we may go;
and heaven is nearer than we think
here in this world below.

He dreamed an angel ladder
stretching to the sky
and saw that heaven was only
a flight of stairs away.

He woke in fear and trembling,
completely overawed,
and made his rocky pillow
an altar to the Lord.

For God is always with us,
wherever we may go;
and heaven is nearer than we think
here in this world below.

He felt that he was standing
at heaven's very door
and vowed to serve the Lord his God
here on heav'n's ground floor.

Later, Jacob wrestled
throughout the long dark night,
but though it left him wounded
God blest him in the fight.

For God is always with us,
wherever we may go;
and heaven is nearer than we think
here in this world below.

Joseph the dreamer

Genesis 37; 39–47

Joseph, the dreamer,
with the confidence of youth,
believed that all his dreaming
was the God-given truth.
His doting father dressed him
in a robe of finest thread;
his brothers scowled with jealousy
and wished that he was dead.

Joseph, the dreamer,
God is calling you.
He has plans you do not know
to make your dreams come true.

They threw him in an empty pit
then offered him for sale.
He became a slave in Egypt
and ended up in jail.
Yet in spite of all his troubles,
and the lonely path he trod,
he clung to his integrity
and kept his faith in God.

Joseph, the dreamer,
God is by your side.
He has plans you do not know;
he will be your guide.

Joseph, being a dreamer, knew
what secrets dreams conceal.
Vital portents of the future
he was able to reveal.
When the Pharaoh made him Governor
Joseph came to understand
his dreams were part and parcel
of the fate of Egypt's land.

Joseph, the dreamer,
God has brought you here.
He had plans you did not know;
now he makes them clear.

Continued overleaf

Joseph, Egypt's master
and dispenser of her wealth,
was raised to this high office,
to save the nation's health.
His brothers stood around him,
and begged for precious grain;
then Joseph knew his private dreams
were part of a greater aim.

Joseph, the dreamer,
God was calling you.
He had plans you did not know
until your dreams came true.

Middle-aged Moses

Exodus 3:1-12

Middle-aged Moses,
hiding in the desert,
trying to forget
the dreams of his youth.

Once he was on fire,
once he burned with passion;
now he has extinguished
the painful flame of truth.

Sitting in the wilderness,
married to security,
wasting his days
on another man's sheep;
far from the suffering,
far from the slavery,
far from his brothers
in an aimless sleep.

But then comes the burning,
then comes the fire,
blazing in the bush's
inextinguishable flame.

His vision is rekindled
his calling reasserted,
as he rises to God's challenge
and a never-dying fame.

At the Red Sea

Exodus 14:10-15

When the people looked behind them
and saw Pharaoh's hosts draw near,
they turned to the prophet Moses,
and cried out in their fear:
'We were better off in Egypt,
we were better off as slaves,
than buried in the desert sand
or drowned in the Red Sea's waves.
If freedom can offer us nothing but death
what is it worth, we say?
Let us return to the life that we knew
in the land of yesterday.'

Then Moses said to the people,
'Stand firm, and don't be afraid;
the Lord who has brought us this far
will surely come to our aid.
The Egyptians you see behind you
may look like unbeatable men,
but when the Lord has done his work
you'll never see them again.
You've only just tasted the freedom of God,
you haven't yet had your fill.
Trust in the Lord who is with us today –
you only have to be still.'

But then the Lord said to Moses,
'Why do my people cry out?
They know the way I've led them,
so why do they stand and doubt?
Forget the false memories of Egypt;
it wasn't as good as they say.
Face up to the call of the future.
Go forward! there's no other way.'

So Moses walked down to the edge of the sea;
at God's word, he stretched out his hand.
A wind from the east blew the waters right back
and the people went through on dry land.

To live in the past is to live with the dead,
to be captives of things that have gone.
But tomorrow is full of the promise of God
and today is our chance to move on.

The Ten Commandments

Exodus 20:1-17; Deuteronomy 5:1-21

1. I am the Lord your God,
   who gave you freedom from slavery
   and brought you into being as a people.
   There is no other God. Worship only me.

   Never think that because I am the only God, you are the only people. I am the God of all peoples everywhere.

2. Do not invent lesser gods to worship,
   whether of wood or stone,
   whether objects or creatures
   whether ideas or people.
   If you turn from me to them
   you are asking for trouble,
   for I alone am the source
   of your life and well-being.

If it helps you to try and picture me, remember that I am present in goodness, beauty and love wherever they are found.

3. Do not take my name lightly.
   You abuse it at your cost.

   Never treat the things of the spirit with contempt. They are the very basis of your being.

4. Remember the day of rest;
   not only for yourself,
   but for the sake of your family,
   your colleagues, your employees,
   and the good of my creation.

   Remember also the days of work. Use them creatively for the good of the community and the health of the planet earth.

5. Respect your father and your mother,
   so that your family life may flourish.

   Nurture all the children, that they may grow strong in body, mind and spirit, and learn how to love.

6. Do not commit murder.

   All life is precious. Treat it with due care.

Continued overleaf

7. Do not commit adultery.

   Lifelong marriage is one of my best ideas. Do nothing to damage it. Do everything you can to sustain it.

8. Do not steal.

   The wealth of the world is for the good of the world. Enjoy the wealth you have, but learn the art of giving and sharing.

9. Do not spread evil gossip about your neighbour.

   Speak about others as you would like them to speak about you. Or say nothing at all.

10. Do not look at your neighbour's life and possessions through jealous, greedy eyes.

    Be yourself, and make the very best of what you have and are. Only you can do that. Value your uniqueness.

The Ten
Commandments

Not bread alone

Deuteronomy 8:1-10

Israel in the wilderness,
was fed by God
with manna for her daily bread
and quails at evening time
for unexpected meat.

Her thirst was quenched
with water from the rock;
her clothes untorn,
unbruised her feet.
For God was teaching her
to trust his word
and not depend for life
on bread alone.

We also wander in a wilderness;
We hunger and we thirst
for that which satisfies,
but, spurning heavenly gifts,

we seek not bread alone
but clutch at golden promises,
which only prove to be
the stomach-churning ash
of empty lies.

Weighed down beneath our loads
of hoarded goods,
we stumble on towards our vision
of the promised land.
But soon our light is spent,
our dream turns mirage
and our strength is drained and lost
beneath the sand.

God give us strength
to brave the desert storms.
Give us your word of hope
which stands
when all seems lost.
God give us light
that shines best
when the night is darkest.

God give us dreams
that do not melt away
like morning frost.
These are our deepest needs,
which only you can meet.
Give us the Bread of Life
that we may eat
and live.

The prophets of God

1 Kings 18; Amos 5:10-24; Hosea 2;
Jeremiah 31:31-34; Ezekiel 37:1-14

God's prophets are the ones who hear and see
when all around them are both deaf and blind.
They doggedly continue to believe
when doubt enfeebles every other mind.
The prophets of the Lord are flames of hope
in dreary days of dark and cold despair.
They are the ones who take the side of love,
when hate and fear and cries for swift revenge
like ghastly demons infiltrate the air.

In times of drought, official prophets fail
to rouse the gods and check the nation's vice;
but bold Elijah simply kneels in prayer
and fire from heav'n lights up his sacrifice.

And later, when he fled the wicked queen,
and ran to distant Sinai's holy hill,
he heard, after the wind, earthquake and fire,
the awesome whisper of God's righteous will.

When false religion dulls the people's soul
the poor are crushed by wealth's unfeeling hand;
but Amos cries, 'Let streams of justice flow!'
and warns of judgement on the stubborn land.

Hosea's love for his unfaithful wife
led him to understand God's own deep ache
to bind his faithless people with love's cords –
cords which, unlike his heart, would never break.

Sad Jeremiah warned of coming doom,
and yet he dreamed that when the worst was done
the Lord would write a covenant on the heart
to replace that which had been carved in stone.

Ezekiel saw a valley full of bones,
and thought of exiled Israel's shrivelled hope;
but, prompted by the living word of God,
he called on Spirit's breath to raise them up.

O Lord, when we are lost in faithless wrong
and cannot see beyond our present pain,
help us look up with prophets' eyes and see
your future, full of light and hope again.

A prophet in Babylon

Isaiah 40; Psalm 137:1-6

By what surprising grace
did this lone prophet,
exiled in Babylon,
have the faith
to see the God of Israel
not as the defeated God
of a defeated people,
but as the Lord of all?

Did he not see around him
all the glory and the grandeur
that was Babylon –
the wealth and splendour
of her palaces and temples
and the famous gardens?

Was he not impressed
by all the pomp and dignity,
the might and majesty
of emperors and kings?

Did he not understand
that God's own Jerusalem
and holy sanctuary
were nothing now but dust,
while his decimated people
bowed in subjection
to a foreign law?

What miracle of faith
enabled him to see
the gods of Babylon
as painted wooden idols
wobbling on their stands,
compared to Israel's living God,
whose breath shakes nations
and whose power compels the stars?

The ragged exiles
hung their harps upon the trees
and had no heart for song;
but this lone, unnamed prophet
heard the music of the Lord
in an alien land,
and could not help but sing
of God's inevitable victory –
'Take comfort from your everlasting God,
he knows your plight;
he comes to take you home.

Continued overleaf

He does not lack in power –
he made the world!
He gives his strength
to those who tire and fall.
And those who trust and wait
will rise renewed.
They'll walk and run;
on eagles' wings they'll soar.
For though the grass may wither, flowers fade,
the word of God endures for evermore.'

Chariots of fire

2 Kings 6:11-17

Elisha's servant watched,
as hostile forces gathered round
the threatened city.
Filled with fear, he ran
to tell the prophet,
saying, 'Master, we are lost;
what can we do,
who are so few,
against so many?'
Elisha's face showed
neither fear nor pity
as he answered, simply,
'More there are with us
than are with them.'

And, bowing low, he prayed,
'Lord God,
open my servant's eyes
that he may see.'
And when the servant's eyes were opened
he could see the hillside
all around his master
filled with horses
and with chariots of fire.

Lord, in those bleak and sombre times
when all the news we hear is bad,
and everything that's good
seems to be threatened
by relentless regiments of evil;
when those who struggle for the right
seem weak
and in real danger
of being overwhelmed –
Lord, in such times
open our eyes to see
that there are more with you
than with your foes.

Show us the unseen power at work
in those who love the right
and stand for justice
and for peace;
whose public service,
gentle care
and unregarded duties,
help maintain the common good.

Continued overleaf

And when the daily benefits
we take for granted
are despised by those
who only would destroy;
give us the grace and courage
to defend the best.
Before it is too late,
Lord, open our blind eyes
that we may see.

And when the powers of dark
so fill the air,
that all seems lost,
Lord, help us to look up
and see the stars
still shining brightly
in the midnight sky,
like heavenly
chariots of fire
ablaze with hope.

Where can wisdom be found?

Job 28:12-28

Where can wisdom be found?
And where is the source of understanding?
No one knows the way to it.
It isn't to be found in the land of the living –
not even in the letters to *The Times*,
or the leaders in *The Daily Telegraph*;
The Sun knows nothing of it,
and *The News of the World* has not exposed it.
We examine the files of the statisticians
and say, 'It is not in them'.
We read the latest Government reports,
but they do not satisfy our searching.
Fists full of dollars cannot buy it,
nor can it be exchanged for hoards of gold.
Sotheby's haven't put it up for auction,
nor is it offered as a quiz-show prize.

Where, then, does wisdom come from?
And where is the source of understanding?
No creature on earth has seen it,
and it is hidden from the birds of the air.
Astronauts haven't discovered it in outer space,
and psychoanalysts have not met it
as they plumbed the inner depths.

But God understands the way to wisdom.
He alone knows its source.
For he can see to the ends of the earth
and surveys everything under the heavens.
When he set in place the cosmic laws,
and balanced the forces of the universe,
then he declared his understanding
and revealed the wonder of his ways.
And now he says to all mankind,
'Consider this:
a sense of wonder is wisdom,
and to depart from evil,
that is understanding.'

Green are the pastures

Psalm 23

Green are the pastures of God's peace;
still are the waters of his comforting.
His streams renew the springs within my heart;
his Spirit satisfies my deepest needs.

Right are the footpaths where God leads;
high are the mountains of his holiness.
Through darkest valleys I am not afraid;
his presence keeps me safe along his way.

Glad is the everlasting home;
rich is the table of God's welcoming.
My vessel overflows with God's rich wine:
goodness and mercy now and evermore.

The pilgrims' prayer

Psalm 23; John 11:14; 14:6

We thank you, Lord,
for this amazing journey of life,
this pilgrimage through time,
which is so full of the unexpected.
We thank you that we do not travel alone,
but we have each other with whom to share
both the joys and the sorrows.
And you are with us to guide, to support,
to encourage and to strengthen on the way.
Lord, help us to know that
in all the circumstances of our lives
you are the Good Shepherd who walks with us.

When we are weak and weary,
make us to lie down in green pastures.
When we are anxious and afraid,
lead us beside still waters and restore our souls.
When we are confused and lost,
show us the way.
When, in our busyness,
we forget you, and wander away,
do not forget us, but come and seek us out.
When, in our foolishness and selfishness,
we are tempted to go astray,
bring us back to the right path.
When we face the valley of shadows,
be with us to bring us safely through.
On every step of our pilgrimage through life and death
help us to put our trust in you,
our sure and loving shepherd,
companion and friend,
through Jesus Christ our Lord.
Amen.

Be still

Psalm 46:10; 1 Kings 19:11, 12

Learn to be still, be still within,
and you will know that I am God.

Lord our God, how can we know you,
how discern your righteous will,
when your voice is drowned and silenced
by a world that's never still?
We are deafened by the roaring
of our ever-rolling wheels,
and the screaming of our music
drowns the sigh of your appeals.
For our minds are sore bewildered
by the newsworld's ceaseless chatter.
And our bodies are exhausted
by life's unrelenting clatter.

Then be still, be still within,
and you will know that I am God.

Lord our God, how can we hear you
through the storms of hate and pain?
Can the whisper of your mercy
rise above sin's hurricane?
For our ears ring with the thunder
of the beating drums of war,
and the engines of man's vengeance
shake the earth and fill the air.

You can hear me, if you listen,
with your hearts in tune with mine,
for beneath the sounds which deafen
lies the Spirit's secret sign.
For I speak in voiceless suffering,
in the tears of the distressed;
and I speak in aweful silence
through the eyes of the oppressed.

So, be silent, all you nations,
and be still, all humankind.
I am with you in the earthquake,
in the fire and in the wind.
But my Way is love, not hatred,
and I work with gentle power,
in the courage and compassion
of the servants of the poor.

Continued overleaf

And to you who learn to listen
I will speak with words of peace.
I will be your strength and refuge,
until wind and fire shall cease.

So be still, and you will know;
be truly still and you will know
that I am God.

Sing a new song

Psalm 96 and Psalm 98

Sing a new song to the Lord –
not the old song of vengeance and hate,
the raucous shout of xenophobia,
the bitter lament of prejudice and fear,
nor the strident cry of racial discord
and the stiff-jawed growl
of unrelenting power.

But let the world resound
with the music of hope,
and thrill to the harmonies
of reconciliation.
Let the whole earth sing
the soothing melody of mercy,
until the air is filled
with the voices of thanksgiving
and all life beats
to the rhythm of our God.

Phoning home

Psalm 130:1-6

I'm here, Lord.
Can you hear me?
I'm lost, Lord,
in an alien world,
like a drop-out from heaven.
I've fallen from the light
into the darkness
and the clouds of glory have long gone.
I'm phoning home because
I need to hear a friendly voice,
some reassurance, comfort, hope,
some guidance and advice – anything.
I need to know you're still there
and that you know I'm here,
lonely and afraid.

Answer me, Lord.
I'm holding the receiver to my ear.
Can you hear the tone?
It's urgent, Lord.
I'm waiting, Lord.
Can't you hear it ringing,
ringing, ringing, ringing, ringing . . . ?

All creation, praise the Lord

Psalm 148

Praise the Lord!

Praise him, all you heavenly angels.
Praise him, beings in outer space.
Praise him, galaxies and planets,
blazing sun and moon's bright face.

All creation, praise the Lord,
for he formed you by his word.

Praise him, all you varied weathers:
rain and sunshine, frosts and snows
praise him, lightning, praise him, thunder,
praise him, every wind that blows.

All creation, praise the Lord,
for he formed you by his word.

Praise him, all his green creation,
plants and hedgerows, flowers, and trees;
filling earth with wealth and beauty,
bearing fruit your God to please.

All creation, praise the Lord,
for he formed you by his word.

Praise him, all you living creatures
in the sea, the earth, the sky;
swimming, creeping, running, flying,
praise the Lord your God on high.

All creation, praise the Lord,
for he formed you by his word.

Praise him, people of all ages,
rich and poor and weak and strong.
Praise the Lord your God who made you;
join together in this song:

God is great, there is none greater!
Praise his name all heaven and earth;
for he reigns through all creation,
brings all things that are to birth!

One day

Isaiah 2:4; Micah 4:3, 4; Isaiah 11:6-9;
Leviticus 25:8-12; Revelation 21:1, 4

One day
the world will live in peace,
for God will settle our disputes
and we shall beat our swords to ploughs
and turn our spears to pruning hooks;
for nation will no longer fight
with nation, and will learn no more
the cruel strategies of war,
but everyone will live secure
and free from fear –
one day.

One day
the earth will be renewed,
and harmony will reign
among all living things;

and wolf and leopard, lamb and goat
shall live in peace,
while children play
and meet no harm
from deadly snake
or roaring lion;
for none shall hurt
and none destroy
in all the land;
and as the waters fill the sea
so shall the knowledge
of the Lord our God
fill all the earth –
one day.

One day
all those who live and work
like slaves
shall be set free,
debts cancelled,
land restored,
in that great triumph of the Lord,
the year of Jubilee,
when there's an end to death
and grief and pain
when every tear is wiped away –
one day.

Let us then play our part
by getting ready for that day
with all our heart –
today.

An Advent prayer

Isaiah 9:2

Eternal Father,
we thank you for this Advent season of hope and expectation.
We thank you that,
even in these dark days of approaching winter,
we can celebrate the coming of the light.

O Lord of light and truth:
shine in our darkness.

We thank you for the life of Jesus Christ,
and the light of goodness
which he brought into the world.
We thank you that his light has inspired prophets and saints in every generation
to overcome the darkness of hate, fear, greed, lust and callous indifference
with the radiance of love, faith, generosity, kindness and compassion.

May that same radiance enlighten this present age.
We pray for children abused and neglected,
for refugees fleeing from persecution,
for ethnic minorities who are victims of racism,
for bitter, damaged people seeking dangerous refuge
in drugs, alcohol or violence against others.

O Lord of light and truth:
shine in our darkness.

We thank you for the Gospel of Jesus Christ,
which gives hope of the coming of your kingdom.
Give the light of hope to those who live in the darkness
of conflict, poverty and oppression.
Give the light of hope to those who labour
for peace, justice and human dignity.
We pray for those who seek reconciliation between . . .,
who work for peace in . . .,
who give their services
to those who are hungry and deprived,
in cities and villages across the world.

O Lord of light and truth:
shine in our darkness.

We thank you for the Spirit of Jesus Christ,
which shines wherever there is compassion, forgiveness
and healing.

Continued overleaf

Holy Spirit, shine even in our lives,
to bring comfort to those who mourn,
release to those who are burdened
with anxiety or guilt,
friendship to those who are lonely,
strength to the sick
and peace to those who live in fear.
We pray especially for . . .

O Lord of light and truth:
shine in our darkness.

Lord, give us grace in this Advent season
to cast aside the works of darkness
and put on the armour of light,
for the sake of Jesus Christ our Lord.
Amen.

God with us

Matthew 1:23

In answer to our searching
and our fear of being alone,
God entered human history
in the person of his Son.
The Word that brought the world to be
was heard in Galilee.
The voice that said, 'Let there be light'
cried out on Calvary.
The feet that danced when time began
now walked in dust and blood.
The hand that formed the galaxies
was nailed to a cross of wood.

For God said, 'I am with you.
I came in flesh and bone
to show you that I love you
and you'll never be alone.'

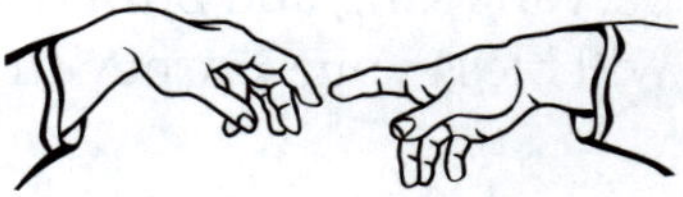

Men of wisdom from the east

Matthew 2:1-12

Men of wisdom from the east
see the light that leads to Christ.
Truth's bright star in heaven's course
will guide you to its lowly source.

Seek him not in royal hall;
he was born in cattle stall;
not in proud Jerusalem,
but here in humble Bethlehem.

Bring your gifts of wealth and power,
gold and frankincense and myrrh.
Servant King and Suffering Priest
will bless your journey from the east.

Do not fall for Herod's wiles,
half-concealed by lying smiles.
Take the truth you've found today
and go back home a better way.

Wise men's gifts

Matthew 2:1-12

Whatever happened to the Magi's gold, Lord Jesus?
Did it fall into the hands of Herod's men,
when you fled from Bethlehem?
Or maybe it dropped off the back of a camel
on the road into Egypt
and was picked up by the greedy fingers
of a passing merchant.
Otherwise, how does that gold,
symbol of the whole wealth of the whole world,
given to you by wise men for safe keeping,
now come to be in the hands
of the minions of Mammon,
the manipulators of money markets,
the profiteers and speculators,
the fraudulent, the affluent and the corpulent?

Surely this is not what it means when it says
that you became poor, that we might become rich.
Call on new wise men, O Christ,
to give you back your gold,
because it's burning holes in humanity.

And what about the frankincense, Lord,
symbol of religion?
Did your mother drop it in the temple,
to be claimed by the authorities
and piped down a succession of priests and prophets,
crowd-stirrers and heart-throbs,
its mesmerising smoke wafting by the nostrils
of centuries of idols,
to the accompaniment of holy turnstile music?
Take back the frankincense, O Christ,
before we are choked by the stink
of the worship of false gods.

But the myrrh, the symbol of death,
and most unlikely of birthday presents,
you did not lose.
You kept it, without ever needing it;
for, having died,
your body could not be found to be embalmed,
and you could not simply be preserved
as a fragrant memory.
Instead, your living Spirit strides the world,
looking for those who are wise enough
to give you back the incense and the gold.

The innocents

Matthew 2:13-23; John 1:10

What do we do with the babe in the cradle;
the babe in the cradle, the hope of the world?
House it in shanty town, hovel and stable;
a refugee camp for the hope of the world.

How do we care for the infant so helpless;
the infant so helpless, the young one so frail?
Give it no doctors, no fit sanitation;
and raise it in squalor, the young one so frail.

How do we nourish the seed of the future;
the seed of the future, the heir of mankind?
Feed it with charity soya bean mixture;
a cupful of rice for the heir of mankind.

How do we nurture the child full of promise;
the child full of promise, the light of the world?
School it in prejudice, half truths and falsehood,
and quench with dark hatred the light of the world.

Where are the wise men with gifts for a baby;
with gifts for a baby, but fit for a king?
Bring him the best of the world's wealth, and maybe
our great expectations will blossom in him.
Treat him with reverence,
the tender young sapling;
then great expectations will blossom in him.

Wild John

Matthew 3:1-12; Mark 1:1-8; Luke 1:11-17, 76-80; 3:1-18

Isn't it time for someone
to shout in the desert
like wild John;
to come out from hiding
in those stone cold cathedrals
and mahogany chapels,
to climb down
from those polished pulpits,
and leave those pre-conditioned
packaged congregations?

Isn't it time for someone
to go out and shout in the desert
like wild John;
someone not dressed up
in man-made fibres,
or driving a limousine,

living on super-bread,
or sleeping on Slumberland,
or receiving ecclesiastical commission;
but someone like wild John,
with a wilderness diet,
and dressed for the desert;
apart from it all,
where he can see it straight?

Isn't it time for someone
to shout loud in the desert
like wild John;
washing the dust off our civilisation,
before the fire comes
and burns up the chaff;
cleansing the dirt
from a sordid generation
in a river of hope,
and bathing the wounds
of the violent centuries,
ready for healing?

Isn't it time for someone
to shout in the desert
like wild John:
'Level off the unjust hills;
fill in the oppressed valleys;
straighten the crooked ways
and make a smooth road
for the Lord to enter his kingdom'?

The Beatitudes

Matthew 5:1-12

In the kingdom of Mammon they firmly believe
that happiness is a cigar,
an expensive meal, a successful deal,
or a luxury motor car.
But the kingdom of heaven belongs to the poor
who want no more.

In the kingdom of Mammon they laugh and they sing
to the promptings of pleasure machines;
they are grimly resolved to enjoy every hour
and perpetuate youth by all means.
But God gives true comfort to all those who mourn
and are reborn.

In the kingdom of Mammon they know how to rule
with arrogant metallic powers;
they scan the horizon with violent eyes
from distant electronic towers.
But God has apportioned this earth to the meek,
who gently seek.

In the kingdom of Mammon they hunger and thirst
for possessions and pleasure and power;
and though the first taste may be sweet to the tongue,
their increase is putrid and sour.
But those who crave good are eternally filled,
as God has willed.

In the kingdom of Mammon the law of the state
is enforced with an iron intent;
the offender is crushed with the harshest revenge
that justice's slaves can invent.
But God reserves mercy for those who forgive,
glad to let live.

In the kingdom of Mammon they search for the truth
in a million mystical ways:
from magic and trances to dangerous drugs,
and the latest nonsensible craze.
But God shines on those who combine a pure heart
with childlike art.

In the kingdom of Mammon they're masters of war
with their missiles and bombers and guns;
they are always prepared for surprising attacks
and the blazing of nuclear suns.
But the children of God are the ones who make peace;
may they increase.

Continued overleaf

In the kingdom of Mammon they torture and kill
for the sake of the popular good;
any threat to the state will be jailed without trial
or nailed to a blunt cross of wood.
But God's kingdom belongs to all those who endure,
faithful and sure.

The kingdom of Mammon looks noble and grand
in the glare of technology's day,
but its concrete foundations are rooted in sand
and are ready to crumble away.
The kingdom of heaven is founded on rock;
proof against shock.

Blessed are the meek

Matthew 5:5

Though proud men ruled the world,
enthroned in pomp and power,
the plan of God unfurled
in a fragile village flower,
an unsophisticated girl,
who dared say 'Yes' to God's strange will.

Those rich men did not know,
wrapped in cocoons of gold,
that, where the raw winds blow,
God's message was being told
to poor men watching through the night,
bedazzled by mysterious light.

And those with earthbound eyes
could never understand
that God accounted wise
men from a distant land,
who searched the heavens for signs of grace
and chased a star to see God's face.

The great ones have their day
and strut this worldly stage,
while God prepares a play
fit for a different age,
when wooden cross and stable birth
empower the meek to rule the earth.

The bank of heaven

Matthew 6:19-21; Luke 12:33, 34; Romans 14:12

If you ever get to heaven,
you'll be shown around
by a guardian angel.
And one of the places you'll visit
on the very first day
will be the Celestial Bank.
(I know there is a bank,
because Jesus told us
to lay up treasures for ourselves
in heaven.)
So they'll bring out your account,
and with a frown and a sigh
and a shaking of the head
they'll probably say,

'If only you'd put more in
on earth,
you could have taken more out
in heaven.'

So be warned –
it isn't yet too late
to start investing.

Contact

Matthew 8:1-3; Mark 1:40-42; Luke 5:12, 13

Jesus was not afraid
to touch people;
not with the formal handshake of greeting,
or the limp clasp of indifference;
not with the vicious jab of hate,
the lascivious stroke of lust,
or greed's sweaty clutch;
but with the gentle touch
of fingers on blind eyes,
deaf ears and speechless tongues;
the touch that healed.
His reassuring grasp
cleansed scaly leprous hands.
His grip was strong enough
to put the lame on their feet
and free the paralysed.

Let those of us
whose fingers touch, not other fingers,
but computer buttons;
who hide behind a barrier
of printed words,
instructions and reports,
or the armchair newspaper;
who never actually meet
the needs of our neighbour,
except through collection boxes
held in the gloved hands of charity;
who are divided from others
by stone walls
or wooden pews
or windscreens
and well-trimmed hedges,
remember that Jesus Christ,
the Word made flesh,
the very hand of God,
was not afraid to touch
people.

Nor was Jesus afraid
to be touched
by people;
not just the accidental jostle
of the anonymous crowd
(though even that could help);
nor the playful prods of children
(though he would not turn them away),

Continued overleaf

but even the soldiers' rough brutality,
the stinging slaps and cold spittle
of Pilate's grinning henchmen;
the bitter kiss of a traitor,
and the burning talons
of the crucifiers.

So Christ's Body still
reaches out to those
who ache for love.
Nor should it shrink back
from the world's unfeeling blows,
but, turning cheek,
use even that as
saving contact.

The preacher

Matthew 13:1-9; Mark 4:1-9; Luke 8:4-8; 2 Timothy 4:1-5

A preacher went forth to preach,
and, as he preached,
some words fell by the wayside
into the ears of casual visitors
to holy places on special occasions;
and these unprepared strangers
could not understand the alien language
of an exclusive religion;
and they remained unimpressed
even by the crushing handshakes
and the hard seats.

And some of the preacher's words fell
among the sedimentary rocks
of conventional worship –
like polished pebbles, echoing and clattering,
and adding another layer to a dead tradition.

And some words floated like thistledown
among the prolific weeds
of humdrum thinking;
they settled, without taking root,
among the choking tendrils
of mediocre expectations.

And some words fell onto the good ground
of minds and hearts
open, eager and hungry;
but the words themselves
were like dry pellets
that even the birds would spit out –
pieces of grit, which sometimes sparkle,
but have no power,
except to blind searching eyes.

And the preacher returned
to his lonely chamber
without even a twofold harvest.

Continued overleaf

'What use to curse the soil
if the seed is sterile?'
God told him.
'Come close to me in life and prayer
and listen for my Word;
look again into the treasury of Scripture
and I will show you seed
potent enough to bear fruit
in all weathers;
and a lamp bright enough
to guide the feet of pilgrims
through the valley of shadows;
and a sword, sharp enough
to pierce to the very heart.'

Welcome

Matthew 13:53-58; Mark 6:1-5; Luke 4:16-30

Jesus Christ is welcome in his own home town,
where we bask in the sunshine of his fame.
He is Joseph's son, the joiner,
and of all of Nazareth's lads
he's the only one who ever made a name.
We will rest on his laurels;
we will gloat on his success,
as the tourists flock the market,
as the crowds begin to press;
and when Jesus has passed on
we'll still sell Jesus souvenirs;
he's the best thing that has happened
in a thousand million years.

Jesus Christ is welcome in his own home town,
when he worships with us on the sabbath day.
Our habitual religion
gets a comfortable boost
with the presence of our hero while we pray.

He supports our age-old customs,
he reveres our hallowed ways,
as he reads the ancient prophet,
as he speaks of better days.
He will help defend morality,
make decent people glad.
He will keep this town respectable;
our own dear village lad.

But Jesus isn't welcome in his own home town,
when he starts to pass harsh judgement on his kin.
It is one thing to inspire us
with his gracious words of hope,
quite another to accuse us all of sin.
How dare he come among us
making wild, outrageous claims?
He was brought up in the alleys
where we played our childhood games.
Does this upstart think he's better
than the folk he's left at home?
Then we'll cast him out for evermore!
We'll give him 'kingdom come'!

So Jesus passed among them
and went on his lonely way,
shaking all the dust of bitterness from his feet.
But the prejudice and fear
which sought his blood
were not content
until they'd driven him from *every* lane and street.

Continued overleaf

And outside a city wall
he was excluded from that place,
and was forced to die with criminals
in shame and in disgrace.
But he's opened up a kingdom
filled with God's unbounded grace
in which welcome for the outcast
is complete.

Therefore Jesus Christ will welcome
to his own home town
every sad and weary stranger,
every child laid in a manger,
every friendless, homeless creature,
every wandering, love-filled preacher,
all who suffer dreadful loss,
all who end up on a cross;
and their joy will banish gloom
when they rise up from the tomb
in the kingdom of the Lord,
which is their home.

Enough

Matthew 14:15-21; Mark 6:35-44; Luke 9:12-17; John 6:5-13

When Jesus asked his friends
to feed the hungry crowd,
they said,
'It's far too late today;
we can't afford to pay;
let's send them all away
to feed themselves.'

But Jesus answered,
'No. You will not need a lot.
Find out how much you've got.'

They came again to him and said,
'We've only found two fish
and these five loaves of bread;
but what's the use of them
among so many?'

Jesus replied,
'It is enough. You need
no more than this to feed
these hungry people.'

However big your task,
if only you will ask,
you're sure to find enough –
enough to start with.

They gave him what they had
and he looked up to heaven,
giving thanks to God.
And then he told his friends
to share the food
among the people
sitting on the ground;
and that's when,
to their great surprise,
they found
there was enough
to go around.

However big your task,
if only you will ask,
God will provide enough
to go along with.

Continued overleaf

After the people had been fed,
the friends of Jesus
picked up all the pieces
of the fish and bread
that were left over,
so that nothing
should be wasted,
and they filled
twelve baskets
with the food
that people
had not even tasted.

However big your task,
if only you will ask,
God gives you more than enough,
to finish with.

Transfiguration

Matthew 17:1-20; Mark 9:2-29; Luke 9:28-43

The mountain flames with light
as Christ, heaven's window,
opens this dark world
to divine glory.
He glows with a strange radiance
normally hidden
from earthbound eyes,
but now revealed
to dull disciples
facing the unknown.

And meanwhile,
down in the valley,
not lit by other worlds,
untransfigured suffering
distorts humanity.

Wretched bearers of pain
cry out for healing.
Well-meaning helpers
offer ineffectual suggestions,
while bystanders move in
with trivial objections.
Unillumined disciples
fail
and turn away,
embarrassed and ashamed.
Is their faith
not even the size
of a mustard seed?

Our earthly light is not enough,
unless transfigured
by the light from heaven.
Thank God that Christ's true glory
was not left to be enshrined
on some irrelevant mountain top;
but he came down
into the valley
to embrace the human beast
with arms stretched out
in sacrificial love,
that we might share
his royal beauty,
and dark earth at last
be radiant with heaven.

Lord, you are all around us

Matthew 18:20

Lord, you are all around us.
Open our eyes to see –
in star and mountain, sun and snow;
in ocean, flower and tree.

Lord, you are all around us.
Help us to understand –
in speech and music, book and poem;
in artist's brush and hand.

Lord, you are all around us.
Give us the faith to know –
in prayer and worship, bread and wine;
in cross and candle glow.

Lord, you are all around us.
Fill us with love to care –
for friend and family, stranger and foe;
our neighbours everywhere.

Lord, you are deep within us.
Move us to live for you –
give strength and courage, hope and peace,
in all that we are and do.

Lord, you are close beside us.
Lead us in paths of right –
through joy and sorrow, laughter and tears,
journeying to the light.

children come

13-15; Mark 10:13-16; Luke 18:15-17

When mothers brought their children
to sit on Jesus' knee,
his followers turned them all away;
said, 'We've no time to stop and play;
we're doing kingdom work today;
go home and let us be.'

When Jesus saw the children,
he called them to his side;
he said, 'The kingdom is your home,
and those who want to enter in,
must all, like you, be born again
and leave behind their pride.'

When children came to Jesus,
they did not understand
the language of theology,
or sound ecclesiology –
they came without apology
and took him by the hand.

So Jesus blessed the children
and put them in our care,
that we might save and not destroy,
and nurture goodness, hope and joy
in every girl and every boy
till love reigns everywhere.

Three cheers for Jesus

Matthew 21:8-15; John 19:1-5; Matthew 27:35-44

Three cheers for Jesus!
He comes to be our King.
He'll overthrow the tyrants,
and wealth and freedom bring.
He'll outlaw every evil –
all pain and fear and greed.
He'll take over the government
and meet our every need.

Two cheers for Jesus.
He claims to be our King,
but he's striding through the temple
and upsetting everything.
He's scattering our profits
and the businesses we've made;
is he really fit to rule us
if he spoils our holy trade?

One cheer for Jesus.
He came to be our King,
but now he stands on trial,
red with the whip's sharp sting.
With crown of thorns they mock him,
scorned by official power.
He's helpless with authority;
this cannot be his hour.

No cheers for Jesus.
He's surely not our King.
They've nailed him to a wooden cross
while people laugh and sing.
The one we thought would save us
they curse and wound and kill.
Our hopes and expectations
die with him on that hill.

Now heaven cheers for Jesus.
The world has had its say;
and God has raised him from the dead –
there dawns another day.
Disciples stand bewildered
beside an empty grave,
but soon they will be cheering too
the Christ who came to save.

Kingdom come

Matthew 25:1-13

Are you ready for the hour of the kingdom,
when the heirs of God are given their freedom,
and the Lord acclaims those sisters and brothers,
who have spent themselves in service of others?
For the Lord will wipe away all tears from their eyes,
and banish all sorrow and pain and sighs,
and even death will perish in the victory of life
when the kingdom of God is come.

And at midnight, when the voice of the bridegroom
wakes us from our sleep to share in the banquet,
will your lamp of faith be empty and smoking
and the Lord of life say, 'I never knew you'?

For the new world's door will be open wide
to receive those who stand by their neighbours' side
with their lamps burning brightly
till the night gives way
to the dawn of the day of God.

The three questions

Matthew 25:14-30; Luke 19:11-27

And the first question is this –
When the king returns
and asks for an account of our stewardship,
will there be anyone left
with even a single talent in their hand,
who can step forward and say:
'I still have what you first gave me;
not increased, to be sure,
but certainly not diminished;
take it back again'?
Or will the problem be
to find any talents at all,
buried beneath the ashes
of a wasted world?

And the second question is this –
Will the king cast his worthless servants
into the outer darkness,
where there is weeping and wailing
and gnashing of teeth?
Or will he consider it juster punishment
to leave us in the darkness
we have made for ourselves;
and go in search of another world
to try again?

And the third question is this –
What are we going to do
to avoid the other two questions?

A prayer on Easter morning

Matthew 28:5, 6; 1 Corinthians 15:19, 20

Living God, we praise you on this Easter Day for the resurrection of Jesus Christ from the dead. We join with millions of our fellow Christians throughout the world to celebrate the victory of our Lord over sin and death.

Hallelujah! Christ is risen!

Even as the birds and trees and flowers utter a glad song of redemption from the grip of winter's death, so may we add our shout of praise for the light of hope that has dawned upon the world through the triumph of Christ over cross and grave.

Hallelujah! Christ is risen!

We were not there to see the empty tomb, but we thank you that we have our own evidence of the resurrection in the presence of the living Christ. We thank you for the times when we have triumphed over adversity; when the light of faith and hope has scattered the darkness of our doubt and fear; when we have been strengthened and guided by the Spirit at times when, left to our own resource, we would have been defeated and lost.

Hallelujah! Christ is risen!

We thank you that Christ's living presence has enabled the Church to survive and grow through the centuries, proclaiming to the world the gospel of love and peace.

Hallelujah! Christ is risen!

We thank you that Christ still walks the earth, challenging, calling, inspiring, guiding and strengthening men and women of all races and nations to lives of holiness, service and joy.

Hallelujah! Christ is risen!

Praise to Christ Jesus, the Son of Man, born of the human race, who went about doing good, healing the sick, seeking the lost, preaching the truth and inviting all humankind to enter into the kingdom of God.

Hallelujah! Christ is risen!

Continued overleaf

Praise to Jesus Christ, the Son of God, who loved to the uttermost, died on the cross and rose again to live and work among us still through his body, the Church.

Hallelujah! Christ is risen! Praise the Lord! Amen.

The temptations

Mark 1:12, 13; Matthew 4:1-11; Luke 4:1-13

When Jesus was hungry, the Devil said,
'Turn these dry stones into bread.
There's no need to starve when with your power
you could grind these pebbles into flour.
Hear those hungry people cry;
are you so heartless as to let them die?
Think of the world in all its need;
what a saviour you'd be if you gave them bread.'

But Jesus looked in silence
to the far horizon
and saw . . .
you and me, in our complacency.
With our bakeries full of bread,
and our superstores full of bread,
and our freezers full of bread,

and our bellies full of bread;
oven-fresh, ready-sliced,
fibre-filled bread;
and the pieces left over
were gathered up
for waste disposal,
but not for the hungry.
For we had learned
to turn stones into bread.
But we still had stony faces without joy
and stony hearts without love;
while the world was starving for justice.

So Jesus turned back to the Devil and said,
'I will not turn these stones into bread.
For everyone but you must own
that man shall not live by bread alone.
And the only thing that really feeds
is the Word that from God's mouth proceeds.'

Then the Devil tried a different tack
in order our Lord's will to crack.
He took him to a temple tower
and showed him how to get great power:
by throwing himself from this high steeple
he would dazzle and amaze the people,
for angels just in time would fly
to hold him up lest he should die.

But Jesus looked in silence
to the far horizon
and saw . . .

Continued overleaf

you and me, in our credulity;
how we were blinded
by the glitter of our gods,
so that open-mouthed
we could see and believe
anything but the Truth
(which is invisible
and requires inner eyes).
And he saw that
we had great confidence in tricks,
and we unwisely followed the stars,
and we were deafened
by the purring of public relations
and swayed
to the music of mass communications.
And we were the unthinking people,
spellbound
by the charisma of false images.

So he turned to the Devil
and snapped his reply,
'It shall not be my way to lie,
and trick and smile and hypnotise
and wear a conjuror's disguise,
and use the gift of heavenly power
to gain men's praise for one brief hour.
What Scripture says is plain and best:
"You shall not put God to the test."'

But the Devil was not beaten yet;
he took Jesus from that parapet
to the top of a mountain where clouds unfurled,

revealing the kingdoms of the world.
'All that,' said the Devil, 'I'll give to you,
if you bow to me with worship true.'

But Jesus looked in silence
to the far horizon
and saw . . .
you and me, in our degeneracy,
bowing beneath the Devil's heavy load,
having received power to become
lords of the earth.
He heard the excuses of the exploiters,
and the explanations of the polluters;
he saw self-promoting empires,
and self-infatuated tyrants,
and self-justifying politicians,
and self-righteous people
shrugging technological shoulders
at the poisoned earth,
while consumers consumed
and populations exploded
the myth of the world's abundance,
and everybody minded their own business greedily.

Then Jesus in anger,
in red-blooded anger,
cut the Devil down to size.
He glared at him with blazing eyes
and asked him who gave *him* the right
to dole out this world's wealth and might
and call on all the human race
to bow down low before his face.

Continued overleaf

For only one God reigns above;
him only should we serve and love.
'So, begone Satan!' Jesus cried,
'with your foul conspiracies I'll not side.'

Then angels came to help our Lord
with heavenly power to preach the Word,
and live a life of burning love
which all this aching world would move.

The fishermen's song

Mark 1:16-20; Luke 5:1-11; Mark 6:47-51; Mark 4:35-41

We were sitting by the seashore
mending our nets,
just to make an honest living
and to pay all our debts,
when a voice from the blue
woke us from our reverie:
'Leave your nets where they are, boys,
and come and follow me.'

'And I will make you to become
real fishermen for me.'

And when people heard him preaching
the word of the Lord,
they were crowding by the lake side
where our vessels were moored.

Jesus gave us a shout
as he took off his coat:
'It would help me a lot, boys,
if I could use your boat.'

'And I will make you to become
real fishermen for me.'

We had spent the long night fishing
far out on the deep,
and we hadn't caught a thing
and were ready for sleep.
But the Lord turned us back,
saying: 'Boys, just try again.'
And the catch was so great, we
could hardly drag it in.

'And I will make you to become
real fishermen for me.'

We were making heavy weather
caught out in a storm,
clinging fast to the rigging,
praying hard for the dawn;
when the Master appeared,
walking calmly on the waves,
calling: 'Don't you believe, boys,
that God's the one who saves?'

'And I will make you to become
real fishermen for me.'

Continued overleaf

We were sailing with the Master
asleep in the stern,
when the sky grew black and stormy
and the wind took a turn.
But the Master arose,
when he heard of our alarm,
and the power of his word made
the wind and waters calm.

'And I will make you to become
real fishermen for me.'

He humbled himself

Luke 2:7; Philippians 2:6, 7

The newborn king arrived
at twelve o'clock midnight precisely
(Middle Eastern Time),
a rather feeble 4lbs 5oz
(but what could you expect
from an undernourished peasant girl?).
No district nurse was present;
there was no delivery bed,
no injections,
no gas and air,
no shiny, sterile instruments,
no hints on correct breathing,
no attendant doctors;
only soiled straw, and cobwebs,
and staring animals

and a farmyard smell;
and awkward Joseph's shaking hand,
holding a shivering lamp
for the innkeeper's wife,
who was busy
with her rough, well-meaning fingers.

So the new red king entered his kingdom
to the pricking of hay, and the tight warmth
of the long swathing bandage.
There was no dignity about it,
except the dignity that attends
every human birth;
no mystery, except the normal mystery
of a new life; no wonder,
except the wonder of excited shepherds
with half-mad stories of angelic visions.

For God stooped low, and will stoop lower,
even to the oozy bottom of the human ocean,
to raise the sunken treasure
of lost souls.

The shepherds

Luke 2:8-20

The shepherds watched their flocks by night,
and saw angels –
while townsmen, sleeping
in a noisier, narrower world,
blinkered against the light,
deaf to eternal voices,
waking only to complete the daily schedule,
saw and heard
nothing.

And the shepherds,
seeing angels,
did not then disperse the vision
with cool reason,
raising mental barricades

to blot out the light,
but received the message
with unquestioning joy,
open-mouthed,
yet speechless.

And these same poor shepherds,
unembarrassed by the stable
and the Saviour's poverty,
gladly adored him,
overawed by the very lowliness
which would have repelled
those richer in possessions,
but with ragged souls.

So the shepherds,
being ready to receive from God
with honest faith,
were as wise in their way
as the bringers of
gold, frankincense and myrrh.

Nunc dimittis

Luke 2:25-32

Now, Lord, please let your servant go in peace;
your ancient promise is at last fulfilled.
My eyes have seen salvation in this child,
whom you have sent in love for all mankind.
His light reveals your truth in every land;
the brightest gem in Israel's crown is he.
His love will move the heart of all the world,
until his Spirit fills earth, sky and sea.

The boy in the temple

Luke 2:41-52

Beware, old men,
of the boy who asks questions
in the temple.
Beware of his probing mind,
like the prodding finger of God
unplayfully poking holes
in your ancient dignity.
Hide those antique laws
before he sees the spirit
beneath the letter.
Protect those sacred truths with iron fear,
or he will fan them into life
with the breath of his living faith;
and the fire of their knowledge
will destroy both you
and your solemn system.

Beware of this boy who asks questions,
the inquisitive Son
of a disturbing Father.

Others there are
whom you need not fear –
they ask no questions,
but tread traditional ways
like sleep-walkers, blindly following
the easy path of custom,
each predictable today
a reprint of a ritual yesterday.

But this boy,
who so amazes with his insight,
is stirring the dust of ages
with the eternal broom of truth,
for he is God's boy,
already about his Father's business.

Martha

Luke 10:38-42; Matthew 11:28

While Mary sat in quietness
at the Master's feet,
Martha fussed and sweated
in the kitchen's heat.
She was too busy doing
what she thought was good.
She had no time to rest a while
and listen to the Lord.
Giving and doing
were Martha's chosen role,
which helped her think
that she was in control.
Yet in her care-filled bustling
she had found
no real tranquillity –
a gift that only comes
to those who learn
how to receive and be.

For Martha's god
is god of hearth and home –
house-trained, domestic.
Does she not know
the living God,
whose energy
drives all of heaven and earth –
awesome, majestic?
Does she not hear,
within her anxious breast,
his gentle word
to all who labour
and are heavy laden:
'Come to me,
and I will give you rest'?

Easy is the way

Luke 13:22-30

Easy is the way that leads to life,
through the gates of the kingdom,
where admission is free
and the Father runs to greet you with a kiss.
Easy is the way that leads to life,
but few there be that believe it.

For the other way is hard
and seems more fitting –
the way of discipline and self-denial,
the hair shirt and the bed of nails;
the way of ritual and right religion,
fine prayers and costly gifts;
the moral way of strenuous goodness
and careful respectability;
the intellectual way of tortuous reason,
intense debate and learned books
and the earnest search for truth.

But that way,
that broad and steep way,
that proud and noble highway,
is the way that leads to destruction
in the depths of despair,
where all is vanity.

It is the easier way that leads to life:
the way of acceptance;
the narrow way
that allows us to bring no gifts,
but empty-handed
to receive from God.
This is the way of the bird with the air;
the way of the fish with the sea;
the way of the seed with the soil and the rain.
It is the way of the child
with the baptismal waters.
For as we came into the world naked,
so must we enter the kingdom of God,
to be born again into his family.

Easy is the way that leads to life –
if it is easy to leave behind
all the clutter of self-justification,
and enter into the kingdom
with nothing.

The converted church

Luke 16:8b

They've converted our church
into a car showroom.
Jesus has been driven from his temple
by the moneychangers
and car salesmen.
But the children of mammon
have proved more skilled
in attracting the eye
of the passer-by
than the children of light;
for the flashing neon,
is more appealing
than the peeling noticeboard.
The grimy stained-glass angels
have returned to heaven
and this worldly temple
is now filled
with gleaming, metallic chariots
promising power, freedom and delight.

The sticky brown pews,
rigidly going nowhere,
have been replaced
by the luxurious leather
of long-distance limousines;
and all those sleepy sermons
have given way
to the restrained excitement
of solemn sales talk;
while the refurbished vestry
bears hushed witness
to the ritual signing
of new covenants,
opening the road
to a mechanical promised land
by easy payments.
The old harmonium's drone
has been silenced
by the subtle murmur
of piped music;
and glossy brochures,
not brown-leaved hymnals,
sing the praises
of god the machine.

Yet over the entrance,
indelibly carved in stone,
these words can still be read –
'The earth is the Lord's,
and the fullness thereof;
the world,
and they that dwell therein.'

The great divide

Luke 16:19-31

The rich man feasted all the day long,
while the poor man lay at his door.
The rich man's body was sleek and fat,
while the poor man's was thin and sore.
The rich man's clothes were costly and fine
but the poor man's were dirty and worn.
O save us, Lord, from this great divide
into which rich and poor are born.

May we who are rich learn to share our wealth
with the poor who lie at our gate;
and use our abundance for everyone's good,
before we discover too late
that the time has come when the great divide,
that separates rich from poor,
has become the divide between heaven and hell –
and we're the wrong side of the door.

Lord, help us to pull *all* the barriers down
that threaten our social health:
the walls of colour and sex and creed,
of nationhood and of wealth.

Prevent us from turning the human race
to a warring and cancerous cell,
which reduces the planet to nuclear dust
in the fires of a man-made hell.

We've failed to respond to your message of doom
in all that the prophets have said;
but now, in your mercy, you've sent us new hope,
through the preacher who rose from the dead.
May we hear his voice; may we follow his way;
may we learn what leads to peace;
may his beautiful kingdom of justice and love
for ever and ever increase.

The road to Emmaus

Luke 24:13-35

Cleopas
As we walked along the road
with the sunset in our eyes,
all the world seemed turned to blood
by the redness of the skies.

Second disciple
And our voices were low,
and our footsteps were slow,
we had nowhere to go
tomorrow.

Cleopas
As we walked along the road
we were talking of the cross,
when a stranger heard our sighs
but knew nothing of our loss.

Second disciple
How the master was dead
who had offered us bread;
now we only knew dread
and sorrow.

Cleopas
As we walked along the road
he began to speak with power
of the hidden things of God
which were destined for this hour.

Second disciple
And he raised our hopes higher,
filled our hearts with strange fire
and rekindled our desire
for living.

Cleopas
When we reached our resting place
we persuaded him to stay,
(though he made as if to go
further on the dusty way).

Continued overleaf

Second disciple
And the words that he said
as he gave us the bread
made us sure that the dead
was living.

Cleopas
We ran back along the road,
though the stars were in the skies,
ran to tell what we had seen
when the scales fell from our eyes.

Both
And we sang a new song,
as we bounded along,
of the Lord who was strong
and living.

The Body of God

John 1:14; Matthew 26:26; 27:57-60; John 20:27, 28; 1 Corinthians 12:27; Romans 12:1, 4, 5

The Lord God presented his body to the world
in the baby of Bethlehem,
the man from Nazareth – Jesus the Christ.
His feet walked the dusty pathway of God's purpose,
from village to town, from seashore to hilltop,
on mountain and wave.
His eyes searched out the suffering,
the lost and the sinful,
and saw deep down into broken hearts.
His ears heard the cries of the helpless,
the laughter of children,
and the voice of the Father.
His healing hands touched the sick and wounded
and set the paralysed dancing.

His voice cast out demons,
proclaimed the gospel truth
and raised up the dead.
For his was the Body of God and he lived among us.

But his eyes filled with tears
when he foresaw the doom of Jerusalem,
and grieved for the death of a friend.
His hands and his feet were nailed fast
to the wood of a cross
by the hammers of injustice.
His ears heard the jeers of the crowd
and the scorn of his foes.
And his voice cried out in anguish
to the silence of his God.
Then he gave his last breath
as his head bowed in death.
And they took his broken body,
broken like bread at a banquet,
and laid it, with spices, in an unused tomb.
For his was the Body of God and he died among us.

But the Body of God was raised up,
and his friends saw his wounds.
And his Spirit filled those who believed
and enrolled them to serve,
with their hands and their feet,
and their eyes and their ears and their voices,
to preach the Good News, and to live the good life
and to love till it hurts.

Continued overleaf

For what now is the Body of God
but all those who would follow their Lord
with the towel and bowl of a slave,
that the whole world might know
of the strong love of God,
who gave us his body
to serve and to save.

Water into wine

John 2:1-11

When the wine runs dry
at the festival of life,
when words fail, and music dies;
when our joys wear thin,
or old friendships end in strife,
and our laughter turns to sighs –
then come, Lord Jesus,
turn our water into wine,
as you turn the rain from heaven
to the sweetness of the vine;
turn the tears of our night
into songs of the day,
and revive us with your Spirit
as we walk the pilgrim way;
and baptise us with a fresh desire
to love you and obey –
Jesus, turn our water into wine.

When you took your towel and bowl
and you washed those weary feet,
you turned that water into wine.
And when we, at your command,
give a cup to cool the heat,
you turn that water into wine.
So come, Lord Jesus,
bring your heaven down to earth,
and fulfil the ancient prophecy
that at the world's new birth
every tear will be dried up
and there will be no more sea;
for we understand the reason
why such wonders have to be –
it's because you'll have completed
what began in Galilee:
you'll have turned all the water into wine.

Nicodemus

John 3:1-17

Nicodemus thought
that because Jesus did signs and wonders,
he must be a man of God.
But Jesus knew
that even the Devil does signs and wonders
and deceives the world with them;
but the true Man of God
seeks only to do God's will.
And that is something the Devil can never do.

Nicodemus thought
that the kingdom of God was a theocratic state
that would be entered by triumphant processions
of shouting zealots.
But Jesus knew
that God's kingdom cannot even be seen,

let alone entered,
except by those who have been reborn
to a new kind of life.

Nicodemus thought
that being born again
meant re-entering his mother's womb.
(Did he laugh when he said that?)
But Jesus knew
that being born again meant, not baby bodies,
but new hearts and minds,
fashioned by the washing of repentance
and the breathing of the Spirit.

'And the Son of Man,' said Jesus,
'must be lifted up on a stick
like Moses' serpent in the wilderness*
that everyone might see
how much God loved the world,
and seeing, live.'
We aren't told
what Nicodemus made of that.

But was he any wiser,
when he came with spices
to lay the body of Jesus to rest
in the tomb?**
And did he ever meet those
who later found the tomb
empty?

Continued overleaf

Do we too, like Nicodemus,
misunderstand
when Jesus speaks of heavenly things
in the earthly language of metaphor and parable?
How, then, shall we ever understand him
when he speaks the language of heaven
in a body raised from the dead?

* *See not only Numbers 21:8, 9, but John 12:32, 33*
** *See John 19:39, 40*

Sitting by the edge of the pool

John 5:1-15

I was once content
just staring at the waters,
sitting by the edge of the pool;
waiting for an angel
to stir up the water,
sitting by the edge of the pool.

But Jesus came
with a word that pierced my heart;
he asked me a question
that tore my soul apart:
'Do you want to be whole?'
Did I really, really want to be whole?

I was once resigned
to a life without a purpose,
sitting by the edge of the pool;
with a paralysed mind
that didn't want a purpose,
sitting by the edge of the pool.

Then Jesus came
and he got me off my seat;
he challenged me to stand
on my own two feet:
'Pick up your mat and walk,' he said,
and I did, yes I did!
And I knew, within my soul,
that this Jesus had made me whole!

Jesus came to save us

John 13:1-5; Mark 14:22-25; Luke 22:39-44; Matthew 26:57-68; John 18:28-19:16; Mark 15:29-32; Acts 10:39b; John 19:38-42; Luke 24:1-12

Room prepared; disciples meet;
bowl and towel; washing feet;
God's plan ready to complete –
Jesus came to save us.

Broken bread and poured out wine;
holy body, blood divine;
was there ever food so fine? –
Jesus came to save us.

Midnight garden, olive wood,
prayers of anguish, sweat like blood;
he accepts the will of God –
Jesus came to save us.

Priestly pride and Roman power;
soldiers' lash; spectators' jeer;
now has come his finest hour –
Jesus came to save us.

Wounded flesh and flowing blood;
sharp the nails and rough the wood;
he reveals the love of God –
Jesus came to save us.

Linen cloth and borrowed tomb;
spices mask the smell of doom;
earth can give him no more room –
Jesus came to save us.

Empty grave, angelic light;
friends bewildered by the sight;
he has ended death's dark night –
Jesus came to save us.

King Jesus

John 18:33-37

They sometimes say that Jesus was a King,
and yet he had no throne or golden crown,
no royal robes or jewelled ring.
He had no army to enforce his law;
his wealth was not in palaces or lands;
he lived his life among the poor.

But King he is; and though he reigns unseen,
and love's the only power at his command –
in truth, no greater King has ever been,
whose love and peace shall rule in every land.

Thomas

John 20:24-29

If you choose doubting Thomas
as your patron saint,
simply because, like you,
he would only believe
the things he could touch or see,
do not then rest
in agnostic security.
But remember that, in the end,
even Thomas was convinced
by the unexpected evidence of his senses.
And Christ may yet turn
even *your* doubt into faith,
by showing you his wounds.

Second Advent

Acts 1:9-11

Shall we gaze into the sky,
waiting for the coming of the Christ
who never left us?
Do we look to the heavens
for the one who lives in our hearts?
Has he left the stage
of the world's drama
in order to return in triumph
and save us all
just in time?

Or will the flash of his appearing
strike upon our vision
not from the clouds above,
but from the depths of faith and love
in those who already see him?

Holy Spirit

Acts 2:1-4; John 3:8

The Spirit is a lively wind –
breathtaking
for those who breathe
the stale air of mechanical worship;
but for sails unfurled
and wings of faith spread wide
he comes as driving energy,
uncontrollably bracing.
He only destroys cobwebs
and dead branches.

The Spirit is a lively power –
not available
to bolster up our empires,
but unpredictably exploding
in surprising places,

strengthening weak knees
and faint hearts,
and giving secret growth
to mysterious fruit.
He only destroys
the rotten enemies
of our souls.

The Spirit is a lively jester –
embarrassing,
with outrageous gesture,
stiff respectability;
tumbling over dignity
in multi-coloured guises,
impudently prodding
deadly faces
into joy and laughter.
He only destroys
our pomp and vanity.

The Spirit is a lively bee –
buzzing elusively
through our solemnities.
He's not pinned down by resolutions,
but flies in dizzy revolutions
round our cultivated plots.
Sweet gifts he brings
of his own making;
and when he stings,
his heart is breaking.

Prayers at Pentecost

Acts 2:1-6, 37-47

Lord, we greet you, on this the birthday of your Church. We thank you for the gift of your Spirit, poured out upon those first disciples long ago, and present with all who have followed them since, in faith and obedience to your way.

Holy Spirit of God, we praise you that you are present with us in worship and prayer, as you have been present with your people in all ages – around us, among us and within us.

Holy Spirit of God: fill your Church today.

We praise you for your divine energy, ever active in the world, from the first day of creation until now, inspiring prophets and saints in every generation, and guiding your people in their mission and earthly pilgrimage.

So guide and direct our lives, and the life of your Church, today and in the days to come. May we discover your gifts among us for the building up of the Church – gifts of witness, service, teaching, helpfulness and pastoral care.

Holy Spirit of God: fill your Church today.

When the Church seeks power,
show us the way of service.
When the Church abuses its wealth,
show us the meaning of sacrifice and generosity.
When the Church is wrapped up in its rituals,
teach us the secret of simplicity.
When the Church teaches fashionable opinions,
correct us with the truth of your eternal Word.
When the Church becomes apathetic, fearful
or pessimistic,
give us faith, hope and love.

Holy Spirit of God: fill your Church today.

Forgive us when we quench your work by our apathy, self-interest or lack of faith, and help us to make room for you to bear rich fruit in our lives – the fruit of love, joy, peace, patience, kindness, goodness, faithfulness, gentleness and self-control.

Continued overleaf

Spirit of truth, fill our minds,
Spirit of Christ, fill our hearts,
Spirit of power and holiness, revive your Church,
Spirit of love bind us together in Christian fellowship,
Spirit of justice and peace,
lead all nations into your kingdom.

Holy Spirit of God: fill your Church today.

In the name of Jesus. Amen.

An Easter prayer

Acts 2:24; 26:8

Lord of heaven and earth, we praise you
that having sent your Son into this world
to love and suffer and die
for the sake of all humankind,
you raised him from the tomb in triumph
over the darkness of death.

Praise be to God: that Christ is alive!

We thank you for those moving stories
of the events of that first Easter Day –
the empty tomb and the mysterious appearances
of the risen Christ,
reviving his disheartened friends
with fresh faith, hope and courage.

Praise be to God: that Christ is alive!

We thank you for 2000 years of Christian history
in which the Church has not only remembered
the Jesus of the past,
but experienced his living presence.

Praise be to God: that Christ is alive!

Help us also to share in the fellowship of his resurrection
and be revived in heart and mind
by his energising Spirit.

Praise be to God: that Christ is alive!

Lord,
we cannot fathom the mystery of your purposes,
but sometimes our spiritual eyes are opened
and by faith we know your holy presence.
You are greater than we can comprehend,
and yet you live within our hearts and minds.
We say you are in heaven,
and yet wherever we go on earth
you are by our side.
Your goodness stands in judgement
over our sinful lives,
and yet you come to offer us peace,
and welcome us, just as we are, into your kingdom.

Praise be to God: that Christ is alive!

Continued overleaf

Lord, your ways are more amazing
than even our boldest thoughts,
deeper than our wisest understanding
and more surprising than our largest expectations.
We thank you that in the death and resurrection
of Jesus Christ
you have shown us that suffering love
is a powerful instrument for good,
and that the grave can be the gateway to eternal life.

Praise be to God: that Christ is alive!

So then we rejoice on this Easter morning
and add our feeble alleluias
to the chorus of your Church throughout the world
and the greater music of the saints in heaven.
For Christ is risen! He is risen indeed! Alleluia!
Amen!

Prisoner

Romans 7:14-8:2

I am a prisoner in space,
locked in a physical capsule
of body and brain;
reaching out five sensual arms
with cosmic longing,
but grasping little.

I am a prisoner in time,
always losing my bright future
in a disappointing past,
and sooner or later conceding
that my brief appearance is ending
to relieved applause.

I am a prisoner of life,
bound by the clockwork demands
of the daily schedule;
systematically drained
by relentless routine
and timetabled triviality.

But, worst of all,
I am a prisoner of self,
whose dreams are quenched
by the inner nightmare
of intrinsic defects,
climbing the down escalator
with persistent gravity.

Who then will come,
to release the captive,
declaring the year of Jubilee?
Thank God for Christ,
Master of space, time and life,
who captures my self
and sets me free.

The holy city

Revelation 21:2, 9-27; 22:1-15; Hebrews 11:10, 16b

What a surprise to find –
after believing for years
that heaven was like a garden,
a green and fruitful paradise
of peace and beauty,
or like a palmy South Sea island
lapped by deep blue waters
on a beach of silver sand –
what a surprise to find,
that when, at the end of the Bible,
a piece of heaven
comes floating down to earth,
it isn't a garden at all,
but a city.

And with its gates of pearl
and its streets of gold
it seems not unlike
Las Vegas;
except for its size.
It is a giant cube,
one thousand five hundred miles square,
and one thousand five hundred miles high.
It would seem to be
a planning error
of enormous proportions.

This *holy city*, as it's called
(surely a contradiction in terms),
has brought heaven
down to earth
with a bump.

But should we be so surprised?
Does God really want us
to dream our destiny away
in a soporific garden,
(or on a pacific beach)
where nothing happens
for all eternity?
For our idea of heaven
often seems to be
a place of self-indulgence,
and of never-ending pleasure.
But in cities
we have to learn how to live
with other people,

Continued overleaf

in an environment
that's rarely still,
and where there is always
something worthwhile
to do.
For every one of our cities
(even Las Vegas)
is some kind of botched attempt
at civilisation,
and this vision
of the holy city
is God's way of saying
that he wants civilisation too.

Gardens are wonderful
in their place,
but what better place for a garden
than in a holy city?

Lord of light

1 John 1:5b

Lord of light, in whom there is no darkness at all,
we praise you for the morning,
when light triumphs over darkness.

We praise you for the light of beauty
shining in your creation.

We praise you for the light of goodness,
shining in the lives of those who love you
and have learned to love their neighbours
as themselves.

We praise you for the light of joy,
reflected in the singing of angels
and the worship of your people here on earth.

Forgive us that we do not always live in your light,
but in the shadows of our self-concern.

Forgive us when there has been darkness
in our thoughts and feelings,
our words and actions;
when we have been irritable and moody,
and made others miserable
by the thoughtless and hurtful things
we have said or done.

We thank you for those whose light
has shone into our darkness
and shown us a better way;
for those who have loved us
when we haven't deserved it,
who have been patient with us in our faults,
who have been generous to us
in our self-centredness.

We thank you for those whose genuine goodness
has inspired and helped us,
whose courage in adversity has amazed us,
whose dedication to the truth has deeply moved us.

For through them your love has lit up our lives
with faith and hope.

We thank you for Jesus, the light of the world;
may his light be reflected even in us
by the miracle of your grace.

We ask this in his name. Amen.

In God's garden

1 Corinthians 3:9 (REB)

Though I have known from childhood
that many tiny flowerets
grow in our dear Lord's garden,
it is only recently
that I came across a copy
of the Lord's seed catalogue;
and these are some of the varieties
I found within its pages:

Suburbiana Respectabilia
This respectable climber
grows well
in pleasant conditions
and with the help
of a suitable
adjacent building.

Plant in September
and it will blossom at Christmas
and, with sufficient care,
bear fruit by Easter.
Then it rests until Autumn.
It does not easily
survive transplanting.

Grandioso Ritualis
This dressy plant,
which flourishes, surprisingly,
in a smoky atmosphere,
produces flowers of different colours
for every season of the year.
It is at its best in clusters,
which enhance its stately presence,
and its solemn dignity
will grace any occasion.

Hierarchico Administrasis
This pot plant flourishes behind glass,
especially office windows,
where it proliferates
with minimum attention
or encouragement.
The main problem is
to keep its growth
within reasonable bounds.
It bears an abundance
of papery fruit
all year round,
most of which is
entirely lacking
in nutritional value.

Continued overleaf

Pentecosto Dramaticalis
An extremely colourful plant,
growing equally well
in inner cities
or isolated rural plots,
and is also found
in suburban gardens.
Its branches wave wildly
in even the smallest breeze,
making uncanny noises.
Its fruit is bright and tasty,
and is said to have healing powers,
though it can produce
hallucinations.

Pomposa Verbosis
This impressive plant
prefers a high location
in full light.
It tends to dominate the garden
and though its flowers
can be attractive,
its fruit can be disappointing.

Mystico Solitaris
This stark, cactus-like plant
grows well in desert conditions –
the more severe the conditions,
the more fragrant the flowers.
Its fruit is only valued
by those who are lost
in the wilderness.
To others, it has a bitter taste.

Saint
A humble plant
which grows in any situation,
and has been found hidden
among all the plants
described above.
Its simple beauty
has the strange effect
of bringing out the best
in those around it,
and its sweet aroma
fills the air with a sense
of calm and goodwill.

We celebrate

Philippians 2:5-11

We celebrate the birth of Jesus Christ,
son of a carpenter, now honoured as a king.
Born in the night and murdered in dark day,
his light shines on across the years
and searches everything.

We celebrate the truth taught by a man
whose words have outlived empires
and outstretched the wise.
His moral vision challenges the world;
his simple Gospel has the power
to heal and civilise.

We celebrate the love which drove his life,
embracing sinners and relieving desperate needs.
His love burns still in all those servant saints,
whose deep concerns and passionate prayers
are matched by costly deeds.

We celebrate the faith and peace and hope
which Christ has brought
to countless followers of his Way –
a faith which lights the road, an inner peace
which steels the soul, and hope which looks
with joy towards the day.

He did not come to show the light of God
in power and wealth,
but in weak flesh and blood of death.
We see God's light in Christ's humanity:
he called himself the Son of Man
and came from Nazareth.

Our global warming world of fragile dreams
hopes truly for the best, yet fears the worst might be.
May we not turn our faces from the light,
but seek God's justice, peace and good
in earth and sky and sea.

Artists have caught the radiant light of Christ
in paint and music, words and wood
and chiselled stone.
But turning our dull clay to Spirit's gold
is work befitting Christ the Master
Craftsman's skill alone.

Visible and invisible

Colossians 1:15, 16

Lord of all,
we praise your name for your creative love,
from which has flowed the whole miraculous,
glorious multiplicity of things
from atoms to galaxies, from dewdrops to oceans,
from nodding flowers to twinkling stars,
from sparking fireflies to blazing suns.
We praise you for this outpouring of your very self
in the beauty, joy, light and life of the world,
in the music of the spheres,
in the drama of universal history.

Creator of all things visible: we praise your holy name.

And we praise you too for all invisible things –
for what cannot be touched, weighed or measured,
bought or sold,
but without which life would be poor and mean –
for friendship and love, kindness and courage,
generosity and encouragement;
for lofty ideals of justice and mercy;
for reason and curiosity;
for a sense of beauty and a sense of humour.

Creator of all things visible: we praise your holy name.

Creator of all things seen and unseen,
we thank you for revealing yourself
in Jesus Christ, your visible image –
a man of flesh and blood,
living in the world of the five senses,
yet living and dying and rising again
by the power of the unseen Spirit,
that we might receive life in all its fullness.
Amen.

The Bible

2 Timothy 3:16, 17

I do not love this book because it is
black enough to please puritans,
holy enough to scare demons,
thick enough to stop bullets,
heavy enough to squash flies;
but because sometimes when I read it
I am moved
deeper than tears.

I do not love this book because
they say it is the very words of God,
and polish every dot and comma,
like golden ornaments
in an idolatrous temple;

but because sometimes when I read it
God speaks in a strange tongue
deeper than words.

I do not love this book because
the passionate preacher
beats the truth out of it
with his blunt fist
and sharp ideas,
(for some use the book
to support their opinions,
as others might use it
to support their tables).

But I do love this book
because sometimes when I read it
I am disturbed by a truth
deeper than thought.

And when I read of Jesus,
then I know,
that he is the Truth,
the living Word of God,
whose Spirit moves my soul.